Contents

Some words are shown in bold, **like this**. You can find out what they mean by looking in the glossary.

What is a truck?

A truck is a large vehicle that moves along on wheels. Trucks carry goods called **cargo**. At the front of the truck is a **cab** where the driver sits. At the back is a big space for the cargo.

Tanker trucks like this carry liquid cargo.

REVISED AND UPDATED

Transport Around the World

Trucks

Chris Oxlade

Heinemann LIBRARY

www.heinemann.co.uk
Visit our website to find out more information about Heinemann Library books.

To order:
 Phone 44 (0) 1865 888066
 Send a fax to 44 (0) 1865 314091
 Visit the Heinemann Bookshop at www.heinemann.co.uk to browse our catalogue and order online.

First published in Great Britain by Heinemann Library,
Halley Court, Jordan Hill, Oxford OX2 8EJ, part of Harcourt Education.
Heinemann is a registered trademark of Harcourt Education Ltd.

© Harcourt Education Ltd 2001, 2008
The moral right of the proprietor has been asserted.

Editorial: Diyan Leake and Kristen Truhlar
Design: Kimberley R. Miracle and Ray Hendren
Picture research: Erica Martin
Production: Julie Carter

Originated by Chroma Graphics (Overseas) Pte Ltd
Printed and bound in China by South China Printing Co. Ltd

ISBN 978 0 4310 8702 3

12 11 10 09 08
10 9 8 7 6 5 4 3 2 1

British Library Cataloguing in Publication Data
Oxlade, Chris
Transport Around the World: Trucks

A full catalogue record for this book is available from the British Library

Acknowledgements
The publishers would like to thank the following for permission to reproduce photographs: R.D. Battersby pp. **15**, **26**; Trevor Clifford p. **10**; Corbis p. **22**; Eye Ubiquitous pp. **9**, **11**, **13**, **14**, **16**, **29**; David Hoffman p. **23**; Masterfile pp. **4** (Ken Davies), **24** (Snowplow); Peter Sawell & Partners/Freight Transport Association p. **6**; Pictures p. **27**; Quadrant pp. **7**, **12**, **17**, **18**, **19**, **28**; Science and Society Picture Library p. **8**; Tony Stone Images pp. **20**, **25**; Travel Ink p. **5** (Tony Page); John Walmsley p. **21**.

Cover photograph of an articulated truck reproduced with permission of Corbis (Ken Davies).

The publishers would like to thank Carrie Reiling for her assistance in the publication of this book.

Every effort has been made to contact copyright holders of any material reproduced in this book. Any omissions will be rectified in subsequent printings if notice is given to the publishers.

This truck will carry glass bottles in crates to the supermarket.

Cargo is loaded on to trucks. The trucks carry the heavy cargo to where it is needed. Then the cargo is unloaded again.

How trucks work

A truck mechanic, like this man, is an expert at fixing engines.

A truck has an **engine** that makes its wheels turn to move it along. The engine needs to be powerful to move the heavy **cargo**. It needs **fuel** to make it work.

Trucks usually have large wheels so that they can carry heavy cargo.

Trucks have wheels that go round. Each wheel has a **rubber tyre** around it. Small trucks have four wheels. Some big trucks have twelve wheels or even more.

Old trucks

The first trucks with an **engine** were built almost 100 years ago. The engines were **steam** engines, like the ones used in steam trains. Before engines, horses and wagons transported **cargo**.

Trucks with steam engines moved more slowly than modern trucks.

Pick-up trucks were first built in the 1930s. They had a **petrol** engine instead of a steam engine. Today many people drive modern pick-up trucks.

This is one of the early pick-up trucks used in the United States.

Where trucks are used

Big trucks carry **cargo** along main roads. They travel between towns and cities. The smooth, hard road surface allows the trucks to travel quickly.

Big trucks like this one were made to carry cargo for long distances.

Some trucks go through areas where there are no roads, or just dirt tracks. The ground can get very muddy. The drivers must know how to drive safely over rough ground.

Trucks have large, sturdy wheels to keep the driver and the cargo safe on dirt tracks.

Flatbed trucks

This type of truck is useful for carrying cargo that would not fit into other trucks.

A truck with a flat **cargo** space is called a flatbed truck. It can carry almost any sort of cargo. The cargo is tied in place to stop it falling off.

crane

The crane does the heavy lifting for the driver.

This flatbed truck has its own small **crane** behind the **cab**. The crane lifts cargo on and off the truck. The driver works the crane by moving **levers**.

Articulated trucks

An articulated truck bends in the middle. This makes it easier to go round corners. The part where the **cargo** is carried is called a trailer.

Articulated trucks are useful for carrying cargo long distances.

The front part with the driver's **cab** and **engine** is called the tractor unit. It pulls the trailer along. It can be moved from one trailer and attached to another.

This man is attaching the trailer to his tractor unit.

cab

trailer

Road trains

A road train is an articulated truck with two or three trailers instead of just one. Road trains can often be seen in Australia carrying goods and livestock.

Road trains have very powerful **engines** to pull heavy cargo over long distances.

The inside of the cab includes the driver's sleeping area.

Long-distance trucks such as road trains often travel for several days. Inside the **cab** is a bed where the driver sleeps at night. Some trucks also have curtains and cupboards for the driver's clothes.

Tanker trucks

A tanker truck is a truck with a huge **tank** to carry **cargo**. Some tanks can be filled with liquid such as **petrol**. Other tanks carry food such as flour, grain, or beans.

Some tanker trucks, like this one, have more than one trailer.

valve

This tanker is unloading its cargo at a petrol station.

The tank is filled up through holes in the top. After the journey, the tank empties out through pipes at the back. The driver opens **valves** to let the cargo out.

Dumper trucks

Monster dumper trucks can carry tonnes of dirt, gravel, or rock.

A monster dumper truck can be as tall as a house. The huge wheels are as tall as the truck driver. Monster dumper trucks do not drive on roads. They work at **quarries** or building sites.

hydraulic arm

The huge wheels and strong hydraulic arms help keep the truck stable while dumping its heavy cargo.

The back of a dumper truck tips up to make its **cargo** slide out on to the ground. Powerful **hydraulic** arms use water pressure to push out and make the back tip.

Rubbish trucks

Many types of truck do a special job instead of carrying **cargo**. Some trucks go around the streets collecting rubbish. Some of the rubbish is taken to a dump.

Trucks like this also collect rubbish that will be recycled.

A machine lifts rubbish bins and shakes the rubbish from them into the back of the truck. Inside the truck is another machine that crushes the rubbish. This helps to pack more rubbish into the truck.

This truck has a machine that picks up the bin and dumps the rubbish into the truck.

Snow ploughs

A snow plough is a special truck that clears ice and snow from roads. During the winter, snow ploughs keep roads open so that other vehicles can make their journeys safely.

At the front of the snow plough is a wide metal shovel called a plough. As the snow plough moves along, the plough pushes snow to the side of the road.

Snow ploughs must work in cold, dangerous conditions to help keep roads clear.

plough

Mobile cranes

People can hire mobile **cranes** when they want heavy objects lifted. A mobile crane has sturdy wheels and **tyres.** It can drive on roads or dirt tracks.

Trucks like this are often used at sites where building work is going on.

boom

hydraulic arm

A mobile crane uses a **hydraulic** arm to make the boom of the crane longer.

The crane has a boom that can reach high into the air. The driver operates the crane from a **cab**. Metal feet stop the mobile crane toppling over.

Monster trucks

Monster trucks are amazing vehicles. Their owners make them from ordinary pick-up trucks. They race against each other over bumpy tracks and obstacle courses.

Monster truck shows are very popular events in many countries.

Monster trucks have huge wheels. They have strong **suspensions** for landing after jumps. Inside the **cab** are strong bars that protect the driver if the truck rolls over.

Monster trucks can be very scary, but they are a lot fun to watch.

Timeline

1769   Frenchman Nicholas Cugnot builds a truck to pull a huge gun. It is the first vehicle powered by a steam **engine**.

1830s   Steam-powered coaches are used in England to carry passengers between towns. They often ruin the dirt roads that they travel on.

1850s   Steam-powered traction engines are built to pull farm machinery. Similar trucks are used to pull wagons on the roads.

1892   German engineer Rudolph Diesel develops the diesel engine. Most large modern trucks have a diesel engine.

1896   The first truck is built in Germany by Gottlieb Daimler. Trucks soon take over from horse-drawn wagons.

1940s   The first small four-wheel-drive truck, called a Jeep, is built for the United States army to use in the Second World War.

Glossary

cab   space at the front of a truck where the truck driver sits

cargo   goods that are moved from place to place

crane   machine for lifting large, heavy objects

engine   machine that uses fuel to power movement

fuel   substance that burns to make heat

hydraulic   moved by a liquid

lever   rod that tilts up and down or from side to side

petrol   liquid fuel used in petrol engines

quarry   place where rock is dug from the ground

rubber   a soft, flexible material made from chemicals. It is poured into moulds to make tyres.

steam   water that has become a gas

suspension   system of springs that let a truck's wheels move up and down over bumps

tank   large container for storing something

tyre   rubber ring that fits around the outside of a wheel. It is filled with air.

valve   device that opens and closes to let a liquid or a gas flow or stop it flowing

Find Out More

I'm a Great Big Monster Truck!, Michael Anthony Steele
  (Scholastic, 2004).
Mega Book of Trucks (Chrysalis, 2004).
Pull Ahead: Monster Trucks, Kristin L. Nelson (Lerner, 2003).
Pull Ahead: Tow Trucks, Amy Wingert (Lerner, 2002).
Pull Ahead: Trucks, Lee Sullivan Hill (Lerner, 2002).
Usborne Beginners: Trucks, Kamini Khanduri (Usborne, 2003).

Index